MW01293058

Independently Foolish

Career Successful, Relationship Foolish!

Dr. Erika Jones, BA, MPA, Ph.D.

authorHOUSE

AuthorHouse™
1663 Liberty Drive
Bloomington, IN 47403
www.authorhouse.com
Phone: 1 (800) 839-8640

Published by AuthorHouse 05/12/2020

ISBN: 978-1-7283-6057-7 (sc)
ISBN: 978-1-7283-6058-4 (e)

Print information available on the last page.

This is a work of fiction. All of the characters, names, incidents, organizations, and dialogue in this novel are either the products of the author's imagination or are used fictitiously.

This book is printed on acid-free paper.

This book is dedicated to my baby girls, Daizha, Zuri, & Zoey who are my strength, my hearts, and my motivation to live. I can only pray that you three learn from mommy and not be successful, independent, and foolish like I was.

Introduction

I t's amazing how women deal with men that are hazardous to their health. How much love is too much love? When is it time to just walk away? It is going to take a death to occur, for a woman to lose absolutely everything, or for the man to actually leave? Women are the most precious beings in the world and are the first to be taken advantage. Is population the problem whereas there are more women in the world than men? There has to be something to keep women dealing with these low down, ain't shit, no good men they keep. It could be sex; however, you can get that anywhere. I have yet to find the answer to any of these questions but, hopefully after reading this book, the women of today can clearly see when they should walk away and stop being taking advantage. Someone once told me that it is harder to find a good man, than it is to find a good woman. Is this true? Don't be surprised that it was a man that told me that. Many men are selfish beings and their egos are way too high. A man could have no job, no car, and bad credit but, think that he is all that and a bag of chips. In contrast, a woman could have a couple degrees, her own car, own house, and own job, and men feel like that is what they are supposed to have. Women are not rewarded for what they do or what they have. The baddest bitch gets cheated on these days whether they are celebrities or not. When is it time to just give up on a man and say enough is enough damn?

When is Enough, Enough?

t all started off one day when I was bored and decided to hit the city with my cousin. I was recently broken up with my baby daddy and only had one child. I was young, innovative, unwise, and very inexperienced. When I pulled up on the eastside of Chicago to meet with my cousin, I had no idea that this one day of boredom could cause a sistah so many years of pain. I met up with my cousin Sweetie and she was super excited to hook me up. I never thought I would be one of those chicks in need of a hook-up, however, I let the bs go on. I met one guy who was totally not my type and as my cousin saw that I was irritated, she decided to find a better looking friend. She hooked me up with this cat named Mook that I wasn't very interested in either, because he was walking. I gave him my number and decided to go home. His real name was Chris but he went by Mook on the streets.

To my surprise, he called me the next day to ask

me if I wanted to go to the show and since I was dating, I figured it would be a great idea. This man wasn't my typical type. He was a little heavier than I liked and he was a man of the streets, which I never typically date. I decided to let him take me out. What I am trying to figure out is, was this a mistake? I decided to drive because I didn't know him very well. He met me in the city in a two door navy blue, Cadillac Eldorado sitting on twenty Monobloc's. I was glad to see he was driving at least. At this point in time I was 19 and I thought these qualities were attractive, however, it should've been to a teenager. He was 26 and probably had no business talking to me anyhow. I was pretty mature for my age though, so I went with it.

After dating for a few weeks I realized that the lies starting coming in. First he told me that his children were 5 and 6, and then I found out that they were the same age. I also found out that he may have a possible child, which proved not to be his in a later DNA testing. Was I in way over my head? Nineteen dealing with a man and all these damn kids? I also ran into him at a party where he brought some lesbian girl with him claiming to be his baby mama. Is this where I should have ran away or what? He had a lot of male friends and they all seem to be hoes or cheaters. I still cannot see where our attraction hit off to end up together 15 years later. We were definitely opposites!

Mook was a very handsome young man, about 6"1, 215 pounds, with a good paying job, however, his lifestyles didn't match mine and I guess that is why they say opposites attract. I started to enjoy the fast life, the dares, and the fun, not knowing that this same fun would be very irritating to me later in life. I went out with him basically every weekend and tripled or quadrupled dated with all his friends. Each time we went out I noticed there were many different women. This made me a bit uncomfortable because I felt that when I wasn't around him he too was probably with many hoes. Guess what? I was right!

As years went on we decided to make things official. I fell in love with him in a couple years time. I enjoyed the non-commitment until I realized I felt that I was selling myself short. I started getting hunches that he was being unfaithful to me and again I was right. I broke into his voicemail by putting in his mother's house address and heard some things I totally didn't agree with. There was one girl on his voicemail stating that he should come over to her house for Easter dinner. My hands began shaking and I immediately was pissed and broke down. I couldn't believe that this negro could be unfaithful to me when I gave up all my male friends I had for him. Was that a mistake too? His reason for her calling was that he has had that same phone number for many years. Have you heard this before? I sure have. I decided I was going to call the chick back and see what's up, after all, he was indeed my man. She answered and told me that he told her he didn't have a woman. I was steaming then, because I heard this before, especially when we were unofficially together. I was thinking in my head, was this dude bragging? I agreed with the no commitment because I wanted to be free, and that just slapped me in my face. Some good advice to women is to make sure you never agree to the NO commitment because you are definitely selling yourself short.

I let the situation go with the girl until I received a call from that same girl baby daddy. He told me that he is disturbed by his girlfriend going over to my man's apartment. Apartment? I never even knew the bitch went over there. So, of course I called Mook to see why he is such a liar and why is he putting me through so much grief. He told me that he is sorry and that he will never do it again, however, he didn't' have sex with her. Should I have left him then? Probably so, but, I didn't, I decided to give him another damn chance. A month later, I started having a woman's intuition and waited until he was sleep to go in his phone just to make sure he isn't still talking to that bitch, and found no evidence he was. However, I found out he had been texting a new bitch. I was like damn when is enough, enough? Are you going to ever stop this foolishness? He asked the girl via text message to go get a drink and she didn't respond. My mind was in an outrage! I was thinking to myself, I know this negro isn't going to spend his money on another bitch and be a trick. That story ended in another apology and broken promise to me. He said he had bad intentions but, he didn't do anything. I definitely didn't take his word for it and decided to just wait to he go to sleep again in a few weeks to check his phone again.

I decided to check it two days later instead, except he didn't have his phone with him. I was wondering what in the hell did he do with it and I just talked to him before he pulled up to my place? Well, guess what I decided to do since he was drunken sleep? I took his car keys out of his pocket and went into his caddy and sure enough that damn phone was in the arm rest dead. I charged the phone up and went in for the hunt. I saw that the girl did text him back saying that Hell Date is on and that was it. I was disturbed that she even had a conversation with him since he was so through and so sorry he hurt me. So, I called the bitch at 5:00 am in the morning from his phone and she answered and I asked "bitch why do you keep calling my damn man"? She told me she didn't know he had a girlfriend because he told her he only had friends but, was single. I went upstairs to the bedroom and woke his drunken ass up and put her on speaker. I told him what she said and he denied it of course, needless to say, she actually never called back. Why did it seem as though I was fighting for this man that, needless to say, didn't care much about my feelings.

I was so disgusted at the time of this incident and let it go because we were planning to go to Vegas for my 21st birthday, unknowingly that I was pregnant. We went to Vegas and had a blast except for his friends that kept calling while we were gone telling him that he would have more fun if they would have come, instead of me. I was insulted by their comments and since then never liked his friends, but I just dealt with them because he likes them so much. We came back from Vegas straight to an abortion clinic. Never knew that a baby would create so much negativity in my relationship. From the minute I found out I was pregnant at 9 weeks until the abortion, we were feuding. I am glad that we did decide to go through with the procedure because I didn't need any more children anyway, and definitely not with him.

The abortion changed me so much but, what changed me more is how he dealt with his children. He is the type of man that would pay for anything or do anything for his children, however, he was not the typical family man. I did have a daughter as well that he would help me with when needed but, he would not join everyone in as a complete family. This made me very suspicious about his baby mamas. Yep, he had two different baby mamas! Every birthday party the children had would past and he wouldn't invite me or my daughter. This made me not like him very much. He realized I got agitated and started lying to me stating that they weren't having parties, but they were. This would aggravate and insult any woman that is in a so called serious relationship. I started thinking if I should just give up or not get too close to his children.

Independent Accomplishments

As the time went on, positive things started happening in my life independently. I graduated college with my bachelor's degree and purchased my first home. Even though things weren't the greatest in my relationship, I decided to continue with my life and better myself. Purchasing a home at an early age of 23 was one of the best things that could have happen to me. I mean, who would have though this girl who had given birth at the age of 16, would be so far? I end up getting a decent job and continued my side-hustle of sewing in hair. Sewing usually brought me in good money each week and helped a sistah with gas and extra expenses. Mook was good at providing money with bills, and things I needed when I didn't have it. However, we were having bigger issues in our relationship since I purchased a new home. Sometime men want needy women to make them feel like they are on top, but, I have never been that type. Before purchasing the house, I asked him if he wanted to do it together, but, he wanted to purchase a two or three flat to rent out and make a profit. I feel him on his dreams to make a profit but, I wasn't willing to live in an apartment since I had been previously living in an apartment and a townhome. I wanted to provide my daughter with the backyard that I never had.

Mook and I were at war for such a long time from me buying a house. He didn't seem to care much about my house and didn't want to move in with me. He wanted to live at home with his mother until he purchased what he wanted. Is he playing games with me? I know that he wanted to do his own thing, however, I wanted to move our relationship into something more serious and committed. At that time we had already been together for four years and I didn't trust him already. I don't think he thought I was going to be able to purchase a house because he promised me that whoever buys the house first, whether it's me or him, we would live together in the purchased home. I guess he thought that it was a joke because four weeks later after making that comment, it was me.

I gave him a key to my house to help him feel more at home and I didn't know if that was a mistake or not. I wanted him to be comfortable and he can feel free to come and go as he pleases, but, that also could've been a mistake on my behalf and set me up for failure. I felt that since he has a key he probably never move in. After all, he never gave me a key to his new apartment when we were at year two at our relationship. Matter of fact, as I reflect back to that apartment, I really hated it. He always had company over and I found things like condoms and loose micro braids there that he blamed on his friends. Was this the truth? I fucking doubt it. His apartment was like a whore house that he let him and his cronies' hangout with their bitches. Now that I reflect back on that apartment, I am trying to figure out how in the hell did I deal with it? I was even having a hard time once financially and asked him could my daughter and I move in with him and said he would rather pay all my bills because there wasn't enough room in his little apartment for all of us. But, God don't like ugly because all those bitches back fired on him, because one of the women his friends had over, told some guys what he had in his apartment and they plotted to rob him. I'm sure he learned that having too many people over your house is not safe. On the other hand, maybe it was good that we didn't move in.

Getting back on track, after I had been staying in the new house about one year, Mook was subjected to a lot of trouble. One day I asked him to come see me and he wanted to go out and hang like he usually does. He got into a fight and was not only jumped, he was robbed. This made me so upset and worried because I received a call from the local hospital from him saying that he was in a lot of pain and intoxicated. I was glad that I didn't have my daughter that night, because I drove straight to the hospital. I was so glad that I had a fresh new sew in, new eyelashes, new leather, and was cute, because the minute I got to the hospital and told the nurse at the front desk I was here to see him, she pointed me in the direction of three bitches that were waiting too. Are you freaking serious? Why would he call me if he knew there were some bitches waiting? Maybe he didn't know. I went right over to those girls and said, "Why the fuck are y'all here"? I was so upset and outnumbered but, didn't really care. The girls told me the story of what happened, that they were at a party and he got jumped outside the parking lot by like thirty men and they robbed him and Mook blacked out. He went out with his brother Gill and his friend Benjamin V. that night. Which explains why it was three females, one for each man.

One girl came up to me with all his credit cards and his charm from his chain. I asked her where the hell is his new Cadillac, DTS? She said it's still running in the parking lot. The police is currently towing it. I wondered why she would care to be at this damn hospital at 3:00 a.m., however, I let it go because it was time to go see him. The nurse came out and said, "Of you four only one could go in". I wish those females would've tried to go before me. I let them know immediately, I ain't going and that I will come back out and let them know how he doing since they care so freaking much.

The nurse stopped me on my way in and said, "Please miss don't say much to him about those girls in the waiting room. We are not sure of his condition, his head is swollen, and he could have a concussion". I went in and saw that he was swollen like a balloon with a neck brace on. I wanted to cry but, I was furious from the heffas in the waiting room. I did what the nurse said and didn't say anything. He was very happy to see me however, and I don't know why. I wish he would have just come to the house with me like I insisted, but, he must be in the club all the damn time. Did I forget to mention his age? He is seven years older than me. He was thirty years old during this incident and I was 23. Anyways, I took him to my house to nurse him and he of course he was very kind to me acting like he missed me so much. I loved this man, but, he was starting to make me feel like I was being taken advantaged. It took about a week for the swelling to go down and as soon as he was healed and looking back regular, that nigga was gone.

After the jumping incident he kind of slowed down from the streets somewhat, but, I should have known he would return right back. Not that many months later, he was locked up for something he did not do but one of his closest friends set him up. I didn't appreciate the fact that he went through such a setup. The police impounded his car and locked him up. Because he was locked up on a Friday, I was able to go to court for him on Saturday at the county on 26th and California. I was in the courtroom with his mom when they called his name to approach the bench. As I held his mother hand in prayer, the lord answered us and allowed him to get an I-bond due to the fact that he had no record and no priors. I was in way over my head to think that this matter was over.

He went to court for nearly a year fighting this case, and things just seemed to not get any better between us. When he first got out, things were great because he realized after being locked up that I was the one for him, however, he started going out with his thirsty friends every weekend again. This troubled me because I knew he didn't need to get in any more trouble, however, just before my eyes, he got locked up again. This time things were worst. I didn't know what was going to happen if he couldn't get out this time because he was already out on bond. Once you are out on bond, you cannot get into any additional trouble, until the case is over or you take your ass right back to jail. Mook didn't know what he was going to do this time because the judge wouldn't let him out on bond when the bond hearing approached. This was the worst news I ever heard. As tears rolled down my eyes, there wasn't any dollar amount that could save him this time. In my head, I knew that this meant he was in too much trouble. I prayed all night asking the Lord for a blessing because I knew my man wasn't a threat to society and deserved a bond. He had too big of a heart to be stuck in jail. He helped everyone he could at all times. Man, why must this saga continue? It seemed like he just had bad luck!

Luckily, the judge let him out with a bond eventually. I had in the back of my mind that it is a good chance he could end up in jail this time but, didn't want to jinx him. For months he was going to court and there wasn't a solution. The states attorney offered him a year to settle the case but that negro wasn't gone do that. I can't say that I don't blame him.

The Whore House

As months passed, after court cost, and attorney fees, he decided to put the remaining amount of his money into a property. I thought this was an awesome idea because owning property is the most rewarding gift one can give themselves, however, like all things related to him, things seem to go out of control. The day he called me when he finished closing on the property, I was enthused with joy! I went right to Kenwood liquor store to buy him a bottle of Remy Martin VSOP to celebrate. Of course he took the bottle and thanked me but, didn't drink it with me. He went to drink it with his friends. I felt incredibly foolish and unappreciated.

The house he chose to purchase needed a total rehab. Mook went right in to work on the house and I was proud. I knew that great things can happen from this house. Since he had no mortgage, he thought it was a good idea for me and my daughter to live in his house and rent mine out. I thought for a long time about this idea and the idea seemed alright, but I really wasn't so sure it was what I wanted to do. I mean being with him for six years at this point, and not living together was not my ideal relationship. Therefore, if the only way we can live together is if I rent my house out in the suburbs that I just purchased, just to move to the dangerous city, I was fine with staying in my own home. We argued over our houses over and over again, and I knew time wasn't going to fix things. Months passed since the purchase of his home and I noticed that he started having lots of company over when he was halfway finished with his house. I do think it is great that everyone comes over to see the purchase of his first home, however, the home didn't seem too family oriented.

Our biggest problem with the house was keys. He decided that he wasn't going to give me a key to his house until the house was completely finished. I felt that this was some bullshit, especially since he had keys to my house and was having kickbacks at the house now. I kept thinking, am I being too easy on him by not making him give me a key? But, you really can't make a black man do anything that he doesn't want to. So, I kindly asked for a key and was denied by him. I felt so betrayed, so used, and pissed because I gave him a key to my home to make a family and to live together in which we did not. I didn't know what to do. He kept saying I'm going to give you a key next month, then the next month would come and I would still have no key. I decided then to give him an ultimatum. Either we both were going to have keys to our houses, or we both weren't going to have any keys to our houses. He chose that we both shouldn't have keys to each other houses. I was disappointed by his decision, however, I think it is only fair that we both have equal treatment. I hoped that I wasn't wasting my time and I definitely felt independently foolish now. After all this time, I been so loyal to him and he played me as soon as he got put on. Damn.

Eventually after arguing over keys, things got even crazier. We kept breaking up monthly because we couldn't see eye to eye on absolutely nothing. I was beginning to hear horror stories of all the parties and women he let in his house from one of his friend girlfriends. Now let me give you a history on this chick. She and I are not friends, nor will we ever be, but she was very resourceful. She gave me plenty of information and whether it was all true or not, part of it always were. She told me about the strippers, the parties, the women, the clubs, and most importantly "The Lies"! I mean I would literally just have got off the phone with him and after he calls one of his so called friends, I would get a call from her telling me what just occurred. It was a very irritating circle that showed me that men gossip more than women I swear! His gossiping led us to a breakup after running into him at a club and seeing him all over those nasty looking women. It was a huge breakup and it was the longest we stayed apart...6 weeks! During that period, I needed to think but it wasn't possible. We both decided that we would talk to other people. I gave my number out to this one guy just so I can say I did something while in the meantime he was having company. He moved much faster than me. He claimed that he didn't sleep with anyone, but since I didn't believe him, we were right back to using condoms upon our reconciliation. Was this enough or what?

Nope, not for me! It started to seem like breakups made us stronger so anytime I wasn't happy, I would initiate a break up. It didn't matter what the reason was. One breakup did assist us with giving each other keys to our homes, but it didn't help with building bonds together. We were together now 7 to 8 years and we still weren't living together, still not moving forward, and he was still going out very frequently. By the end of year 8 he was freed from his cases and now discussing marriage to me because he claimed I had his back the entire time. Since we were getting much closer I decided to buy him a big birthday present, a jetski since we had been traveling a lot and renting them. He loved this gift! It was the most expensive gift I ever bought anyone. Since I did this I expected him to appreciate it. We ended up arguing more and more over it. Money cannot buy love!

I don't see how we made it to year 9 arguing over everything like who house to sleep over. There was no logical reason to spend the night back and forth while both paying our own lights, gas, water bills, and taxes. One thing I do remember is him asking to spend the night over my house on certain days. I would be like I am going to come over there and he would say no. I would ask why not, and he would say because his brother Gill is using the house this night to sleep with some girl. This shit was insane with me. This house was the true definition of a whore house. It was like he would rent his house out to friends so that they can cheat on their wives, girlfriends, or just to get some ass. What type of situation did I truly get myself into? I couldn't understand for the life of me how I could have such a successful career and such a shitty ass relationship.

This entire whore house situation and purchase on both of our parts showed how we were not really ready to be in a serious relationship. Although, it was more on his behalf, because I would have agreed to living together, but he just wasn't ready yet and he was 35 years old by now. I was wondering at this time was buying the house a good idea or not? Was it enough to just cut my losses and move forward with someone new? Apparently not, because I continued on with this relationship.

Mook end up getting hurt at work one day and was laid off collecting unemployment when he finally started to see how much I was truly there for him. We started talking about marriage more because this relationship was approaching 10 years with no type of real commitment. We went and looked up rings and decided to put one on layaway at Kay's Jeweler. We decided that he would rent his house and move in mine since we selected a wedding date now. Searching for a tenant for his house wasn't too hard as his step-dad helped him out. His step-dad found him a renter and he moved in with me quickly.

Mook was off work and couldn't really afford

much of the bills he created on that house in the hood. When I filed my taxes I paid his house taxes because he was behind. You would think he was appreciative of this matter. He wasn't! All he end up doing was asking for more and more money. I was so caught up with the fact that we were now in a position to plan a wedding I couldn't think straight. I was so happy that he got a tenant in that house and now was living with me, that nothing else mattered. It should have mattered though because I had a $1,000 mortgage and he only offered me $400 a month to live in the house. The money he was giving me paid the lights, gas, cable, and water bill but it didn't provide anything on the mortgage. Was I this blinded by a possible ring and that he got rid of the whore house that I allowed him to do the absolute bare minimum? I guess so because that is exactly what happened.

The Engagement

What engagement? I had none! My engagement consisted of him never paying the bill on the Kay's ring we selected, to the jewelry store actually calling me asking me to pay the bill. What type of shit was this? Now did he think I was going to pay for my own ring? I called him and said Kay's called me and told me you haven't paid one bill since the original deposit. His response was, "Why in da hell are they calling you anyway??? I was so livid that he didn't pay one bill. I was like thinking in my head that he put this ring on layaway to shut me up. I know there are many women who want to buy their own ring, but I just couldn't do it! I just couldn't! So, I told him to just gone ahead and lose out on the money and when he do, he will lose me.

I gave him a list of reasons why he should be glad to marry me like most women. As many years as I said this list, he was able to repeat it back to me because I have said it so much! Well, I spared no time in my recital. Mook, listen I am 28 years old, I have my own house, my own car, 2 degrees now because I earned my Master's degree at the age 24, good credit, I'm beautiful, and I have a great job in downtown Chicago! I am the epitome of independent! I reminded him that I can have any man I wanted, but for some reason I wanted him. I was happy to tell him that I had a small waist, voluptuous breast, nice little butt, my feet cute, my face cute, I have nice hair, and on top of all that, I can cook my ass off. Who was I fooling though? This list was only confirming to me what I already knew. I was begging this "ain't shit" man, to pay attention to a woman who, any good man would love to be with. No matter how many times I tried to show him or even convince him, it didn't work. The only way now was to leave him for good and I built up the courage to do so.

Right when I was breaking up with him, I broke down and cried but this time he agreed to get me a ring I been wanting but asked me to downsize the price of the ring as the ring I chose was way too high. He end up going to get me a ring that was nothing like I wanted, but I was happy to have one. He did not do a grand proposal neither. It was like a will you marry me at Pepe's type of proposal and didn't get on one knee or nothing. So all that damn fussing I did for a taco proposal at almost 29 years old! Was it worth it? Did I get what I wanted? I guess so! I expected the proposal to be much better and I expected the ring to be better as well.

What I expected to be far better, was the man! How young and naive was I? But I guess since I was young, I had bragging rights! I am about to get married this, and I am about to get married that! I must have said the word future husband to my friends to death that I am surprised they still talk to me today. I knew since I had a ring that I wasn't going to be a glorified girlfriend with a ring, so we set a wedding date right away! We selected an October date for the fall of 2014 and the wedding planning began! I had one goal and that was to be married before I was 30 and guess what I did that no matter the cost! How foolish!

There were many things that had to be settled before the wedding. I picked the colors of black and white with a taste of gold, found a venue, booked it, and paid the deposit. Although the hall wasn't the best hall, we were able to have a wedding for dirt cheap and still get married. The crazy part of this all was that Mook wasn't upset nor picky on what I selected. He just went with the flow. I thought this was him being nice! Until about 3 months before the wedding when I realized none of the men got fitted for their tuxedos or anything. I contacted him once the bridal store contacted me informing me of this. This was a good sign that I should have just walked away. I not only had to give him chance after chance, I also got to beat him to the altar.

I didn't think I would have to do this considering he was 36 years old but, I did. It was also issues with his baby mama, well one of them. Apparently she decided she would start tripping out the blue and didn't allow his 16 year old son to see us as well. It got so bad that we had to lie to her about us getting married just so he could be in the wedding. She decided one day to call the police on us saying we won't bring her baby home. When the police came they were looking for a car seat but this boy was 16. They asked him if he wanted to stay and he said yes, so they left. Now that I think about it further, it was more drama being with Mook than I ever had in my life.

The non-existent engagement process was not the greatest. Mentally I felt that since he still agreed to get married that I should continue with the shenanigans of planning a wedding. One day very close to the wedding, Mook said he really want to get married out of town and do a destination wedding. I was yet once again livid at the last minute input when he had all the time in the world to pick things. I informed him that it is very last minute and that guest have already purchased their airline tickets. I was so upset that I called off the wedding and was balling crying on the floor in my living room. This might be the first time he seen my pain, because it affected him that he decided we could go ahead get married the way in which was already in place. Now at this time we were house searching to purchase a newer home and a much larger home to accommodate all of our blended children.

We had a contract on a house in place and although that first contract fell through, I was not surprised when Mook gave his input that he didn't want to put his name on this house too! WOW! When I asked why not, I was told the same exact shitty ass excuse that he used before and that was he wanted to purchase a 2 or 3 flat building. That was his constant excuse so he doesn't combine us or put anything together for us. At this point, I even took a reflection before getting married. After 10 years of dating and living separate 99% of the relationship, we had no biological children together, no house together, no cars, no bank accounts, just nothing!

I wanted to put something together with us as we were engaged. So, I decided we would sell the jet skis since we were buying a boat and make a profit and put the proceeds in the bank account and then each of us can add money to the account. Well, in fact we did sell both Yamaha jet skis and put about $3,000 in a joint Chase account for us to finally have both of our names together. As we walked out of the bank, I felt like we accomplished something finally. In reality we didn't accomplish jack shit! The very next month, I looked in the account and the balance was $2,750 and the activity showed an ATM debit and a Kenwood liquor store purchase. This negro spent money without consulting with me!

I was so upset I called him and he said "OMG I must have used the wrong debit card, I will put it back! All these Chase cards look exactly the same." LIES! A few weeks later I realized the balance was even lower. Once we got down under $2500, I went into Chase and closed the account and gave him his portion and kept mine. Now crazily all these red flags still had my foolish butt at the altar bright and early in November and happy to be there. Well, at least I thought I was happy and one more thing, we had to change the date from October to November due to me calling off the wedding earlier and losing our original date.

This Damn Wedding

T he day before the wedding, our wedding group
was allowed to use the venue to have rehearsal
at no extra cost. I was excited because we both
decided that we would have party buses come get
us from the hall and we go our separate ways. That
day was a success. I really thought the venue for the
wedding was set up extremely nice. The decorator
did a magnificent job and I was impressed upon
arriving to the hall on our actual wedding day. I
was thinking that I probably should have called my
fiancé Mook to ensure he was up so I picked up the
phone and his phone went straight to the voicemail.
I started calling his brother Gill immediately to
see what was going on as it was 12:00 pm and the
wedding was beginning at 5:00 pm. I cannot believe
I didn't reach anyone until 2:45 pm.

His brother Gill contacted me to tell me that they
were not going to make it and that we need to cancel.
On our wedding day, right before the wedding he

would pull a stunt like this! I was so mad but I tried to be calm and tell Gill that he better have his ass at that damn hall and I ain't playing. Gill told me that even if he did get there, he wouldn't be on time and they will all be about 2 hours late. I snapped and told Gill that if he was late, I was going to have to pay extra fees and the pastor would be so upset that we wasted his time. I decided not to worry about it and proceed with getting my makeup done. By the time my makeup was done, I was told that Mook had arrived. I was pleasantly surprised and thought to myself maybe this was meant to be. How foolish was I? Right now just about as foolish as it gets.

I remember getting ready to walk down the aisle with my father listening to this Whitney Houston song and feeling blank but it was too late to turn back now. I was fake happy, I was finally getting married, but was wondering why I don't feel nervous or super connected? I think the fact that at the beginning of the day, I was told that we may have to cancel the wedding is what threw me off a little bit. I had family fly in town and paid money for hotels and airline tickets. We couldn't cancel. Not to mention my dad paid for the entire wedding so I was thinking in my head, who in the hell doesn't have to pay a thing but still get married besides Mook? I made so much too easy for him and regret began to fill my eyes.

No matter how much I might have felt regret or second guessing myself, I still went on with the wedding. I would have finished with the ceremony anyway due to fear of embarrassment and not making my physical deadline. Let's discuss this physical deadline that most women create for themselves. The deadline that says there has something must be wrong with you if you don't get married by a certain age. That age for me was 30. Having that mentality was probably the worst thing I did besides get married to a man that I know wasn't ready to be anybody husband. But hey! I continued on and got married anyway.

Now let's discuss this wedding. Everything was going good until I realized that Mook was missing for many different parts of the wedding. First, was the first dance and my girl sang live for us and during the dance we were arguing. We were silently arguing because it took forever to find him since he was in the parking lot with all his friends drinking. Also, he deliberately was in my ear stating he didn't really want to do this dance with me. I kept saying to him please don't embarrass me or make me cry today. Wishful thinking on that thought alone. The dance was done and it was time to eat. After we ate, Mook was back outside drinking in the parking lot with his friends. Let me fill in some details about Mook. Mook was the type of guy who loved to sit outside with friends and drink until the sun comes out. He has no concept of time or conscious of anyone feelings that he hurts. He drinks in the alley or at his friend's house every Friday and some Saturdays. If you went out with him on a date no matter what day of the week, he will stop at one of his friends' house. He loved his friends! So, this drinking in the parking lot at the wedding instead of being right next to his new wife, at their wedding together, was typical for him.

The wedding planner was so irritated with Mook as well and the photographer who tried to get as many photos as possible. We didn't get nearly as many photos as I'd like. Typical wedding photos like the groom with the bridesmaids and the bride with the groomsmen didn't exist. It was like I was being robbed of having the ideal wedding to just being glad someone was willing to marry me. Made me think to myself like, am I really this desperate? I knew immediately that I deserved to be treated better. My sub-conscious kept kicking in but it was too late. I was married now. I was Mrs. Mook, and no matter how hard things were about to get, I tried my best to make things work out. At the end of the wedding, we took our wedding gifts and decided to get to our room. Mook started being in tuned with the wedding once he was drunk and danced the night away. Finally! By the time he was in tuned, the frustrated photographer left! But, I don't blame them.

We left there to pull up to our suite to stay for a few days. We decided not to do a honey moon that year because we were under contract for a new house. So, we would just stay away for a few days. Well, upon pulling up to our room, Mook sat in the car very quiet. I asked him was he ok and then his drunken ass decided to give me a piece of his mind which ended in a disaster. His piece of mind was to let me know he didn't want to get married the way we were getting married and we should have waited because he wanted to get married out of town. I cried so hard in the car for about 20 minutes before I went into the room and went right to sleep. That's right! No passion or love on our wedding night. I knew then that I was doomed.

The very next morning I woke up to his phone ringing and it was his brother Gill calling asking him does he want to play the game? PS4!!! Did I forget to mention Mook and Gill plays the game together about 4 to 5 times a week and for hours at a time. Mook told him not today but when I get back for sure. We wasn't even married 24 hours and I was the unhappiest wife of all. I felt like that was so inconsiderate of Gill yet, he still asked anyway. That phone call made me feel like there will be no hope in having my new husband attention and I was right. We counted the wedding gifts up and received about $1800 in gift money. He asked how much will he get? That question made me so upset. I gave him $500 and put the rest of money toward the new house. Since my family and friends were more present at the wedding, I knew that most of the gifts came from my side. At the wedding he didn't invite a lot of people but he did have a small family. Some of his friends were upset that they didn't get an invite to the wedding. He told them that he didn't want everyone around his mom instead of he didn't want everyone around his wife. Which was another red flag. Now believe me, I love his mom to death but it would have been nice for him to show that he cared about me as well.

Mook was a momma's boy for sure and he always wanted to be sure his mom was straight. I admired that about him because his mother was one of the kindest women I ever met and she respected me, and always stayed out of our relationship. You couldn't have asked for a better mother-in-law. We never argued or had any altercations like some of the other horror stories I've heard about in-laws. But, when you build respect between both the wife and the mother, there is nothing but love to be spread around and that is exactly what we have for one another. To this day, I swear I love that woman! She treated me with respect and showed love from day one and always prayed for me. She might be one of the reasons why I stayed in the relationship so long. Pretty much the family was a really nice small family. I never had any issues with anyone in Mook's family. He never had any issues with anyone in mine either.

Moving on, after the stay at the hotel, Mook and I went home. We were now newly married and about to close on our first house together. Well, the first house we lived in that was intended to blend us for the first time and our children. I don't talk about our children much because I feel its best I leave them out the story. I want to focus on the relationship and that is it! Children can be a very sensitive and a touchy subject.

We had trouble deciding what house to buy

because I wanted to live in the far suburbs and since Mook was from the city, he wanted to be as close to the city as possible. We compromised on a city in between. A city I didn't want to live in because I used to live there when I was a baby and like most suburbs that is close to Harvey, have pockets where each block could be different. But, to make my new husband happy, I found a house right off the expressway and only 20 minutes from the city. This made him happy and I was worried. I felt since he wanted to be so close to the city and to his friends, he still wasn't ready to be with just me, and me alone.

The Marital Home

Well, as soon as I closed on the house all alone because he wasn't present like most things, he was to the city every weekend. First his excuse was his children until the aged out and moved out the city themselves. His son moved to Bourbonnais for school and his daughter moved to Normal for school. His mother did live in the city and he went to see her every Sunday which was perfectly fine for me. Except he never not once invited me or the children to go with. It was like for years he needed time alone from us at the house and he made a schedule. Friday nights he would hang with friends, Saturday night if he was feeling well, we could hangout, and Sunday is for his mom. When I speak of if he is feeling well, I mean if he isn't hung over. Often times after a Friday night he would be sick vomiting and hung over that I would have to take care of him the next day. Yes, this wasn't my idea a date night. When Saturday came,

I would go get my nails done, hair curled, and be ready. I would buy new shoes and dresses to be cute for him every Saturday for several years. But, when my day comes, he would always say, what do you want to do? He would barely ever plan a date for us. So, his typical behavior would be to pick up the phone and call one of his friends and create a double date. So now he would see his friends Friday and Saturday. He never engaged in having alone time with me unless we went of town and then, it was like pulling teeth to get him to leave Chicago. Even then, guess what? Those friends of his came with us to many vacations.

We pretty much spent our first year doing just this. I watched the back of his head more that the front of his face. He even decided that one night he would drink so much that he couldn't find his way home. His friend reached out to my cousin Sweetie to ask for my phone number because he was so drunk and couldn't drive home. This was insane to me and I guess I was supposed to not be upset that he spent his first night out of many. I tried to reflect on what I got myself into. I was now 11 years into this relationship and only 1 year married. He was still the same drunken ass man he was when I was 19 years old and now I was 31 years old.

I was keeping myself busy by continuing my education and going back to school to earn my Ph.D. and continue raising my children. My oldest was in private high school and her tuition was kicking my butt and my twins were in day care and it was also kicking my butt. Mooking never once offer one dollar on any of the children tuition, daycare, or even my schooling to earn my Ph.D. The only dollar he had to offer was for Remy Martin. That lucky bitch! But as I continue to live with him, I began to start to think of what I did. As you mature, you do reflect more often.

I made some suggestions to improve our marriage such as counseling and we did just that. For anyone that thinks counseling is a waste of time, you're absolutely wrong. Counseling is very helpful and can work with two willing parties. Counseling is where I got my voice heard because I pride myself on not nagging, but that comes along with getting walked over time and time again. This is what was happening to me and I started losing respect for Mook because he was the type of man that was present but absent and that is a very lonely feeling. I saw him every day, but with his friends, his drinking, and his game playing, I was completely alone. I was also alone financially as well because for some reason he didn't feel as though he should pay more than me or even close to half.

When the first mortgage statement came the mortgage on a newly built house that consists of 2400 sq ft (not including a finished 900 sq ft basement better known as the man cave), 4 bedrooms, 3.5 bathrooms, and a 3 car attached garage was $1650. The house was a foreclosure that was built in 2009. It was the best neighborhood in this particular city and very desired amongst many residents. Mook began to pay $800 a month for a couple of months on the mortgage and that payment decreased in four years' time to $500. Let me explain what happened here. We agreed that he would pay gas and I pay lights and we pay every other month on cable. I think he might have paid 4 cable bills in four years' time. The water bill must have slipped his mind because he refused to pay it for some reason and he dedicated it to me. The alarm bill was also my sole responsibility because he kept saying it was an extra unneeded bill. I am not sure why it was unneeded, because the city we lived in wasn't the greatest and have had high levels of break-ins occur. Even though he proclaimed it to be unneeded, he sure was using it and controlling the cameras. For someone who didn't want to also pay the internet bill, he stayed using up the Wi-Fi.

At this point we were about 3 years married when my first thought of divorce came into play. He was paying about $700 a month on mortgage and the gas bill, and absolutely nothing else. He barely ever helped pay for food so I took care of that too. I end up getting a new job and I guess he felt that my promotion was enough to handle everything and so the more money I made, the less he felt the need to pay. Was this fair? What type of man relaxes to this level? Mook! The crazy part was, he was throwing barbeques weekly at the new house and parties as if he was paying like I was. One thing about me is I hold most of everything in until I snap, and when I do, it is just about too late. I started creating mental notes. Mental note #1 was, I need a divorce ASAP because at this rate, he would be the only one happy in this relationship. Everything about him was beginning to be extremely selfish.

His cheap ass didn't want to pay for anything but expected everything in return. He wanted all the movie channels and all the sports channels on cable but didn't want to pay for it. He always wanted me to cook crab legs and steak but, didn't help with paying for it most of the time. Now, he would occasionally offer $20 knowing damn well it wouldn't cover shit! But his expectations was for me to cook full meals. He always wanted me to cook for him. He came in from work looking for his supper as he would say. I am a really good cook and I don't blame him for wanting me to cook. I love to cook and everyone around me knew this about me.

As time went on, Mook started sleeping in the basement. He didn't want to be bothered with the rest of us in the house. He would watch his games, have company over in the basement, and smoke cigarettes. He smoked a pack a day and I have 3 asthmatic daughters and have asked him several times to not smoke in the house. For the most part, he would smoke outside but on occasion he would sneak and smoke in the house. Yes, sneak! It would be when no one was home and it was cold outside. He didn't want to go outside and freeze but for the girl's sake, he should have. I would know when he did because the girls would be coughing all night. I would politely tell him to please stop smoking in the house, yet he felt since he paid minor bills in the house he can do whatever he wanted. This frustrated me beyond belief.

It was always a question of do you love the girls at all if you can do such a thing? If smoking is hazardous to their health, why do it? Whenever he would smoke outside, it still frustrated me. I know it seems like I am complaining a lot, but he couldn't just smoke without littering in our yard. Every day girls and I would see the cigarette butts in the yard. Monthly we would pick up hundreds of cigarette butts and I would be so upset. Even when I asked him to please throw the cigarette butts away after smoking or get an ashtray, he wouldn't do it. So, this was an uphill battle that I constantly lost amongst other things. You would think by this time, I was through with the relationship and realized that things weren't working out. Nope! I signed us up for counseling yet another year.

Counseling would be a serious fight this time because he wasn't so cooperative. I went to counseling with an open mind and ready to resolve our marital issues. It got so bad that, he couldn't even look at me. The counselor would instruct Mook to look at me and talk, kiss me, and worst, give me a compliment. He truly didn't want to do this but, I still continued with each session. We departed the house every Saturday morning for counseling and things still didn't work out. I tried dates, lingerie, surprise trips, vacations, getting rid of the children for the weekend, and nothing ever worked. I began to realize that

Mook had checked out of our marriage. By this time I knew for sure, that we probably would break up.

I started to question him if there was someone else since he wasn't happy being with me. The only time he smiled was when his mom, sister, nephews, or his brother came over. He kept insisting that it wasn't anyone else, but still he couldn't come home by our agreed upon marital time when we hang with friends. We agreed that we would come in by or before 3:00 am and I wanted 1:30 am but I let him pick the time. He didn't get into the house until after 4:00 am and often times 5:00 am in the morning. Even after asking him to be mindful of our agreed upon time his response was that he feels penalized for being married because his other friends that were married could come in whenever they wanted and their wives never complained. Although I didn't believe that because I did know some of them, I felt like this man was making every excuse to prove a point. He wanted to prove to me and to everyone that don't shit change at the altar. Believe it or not, that was his exact wording. I am embarrassed to even share that fact. He reminded me over and over again that nothing change just because we were married. Unfortunately, he was absolutely right!

Mook began to tell me that he wanted to move

back to the city. I was totally shocked. He explained to me that he didn't like living in the suburbs and that he felt that most of his friends wouldn't visit him out in the suburbs because it was too far and after they have been drinking they wouldn't make it home safely. I was so disturbed at this news. Just because his friends were unhappy about the 20-25 minute drive from the city to the suburbs we needed to move! His very best friend only came over twice and that didn't sit well with him. He wanted them to come over and hang with him but they refused because of the distance. It made no sense for us to uproot our house because of his friends. I couldn't agree to that and I am not sure why he thought I would.

Things got worse when the taxes went up on the house to over $10k. That made him ready to go immediately. Instead of trying to fight the taxes, with the county assessor's office, he began to tell me that he was moving to the city and if I don't move when he move, then we will be living separate. This gave me a lot to think about. I knew that I wouldn't want to move to the city and put my children in a bad school or a neighborhood that I didn't like. Mook began pursuing looking for properties in the city that he could buy cash. He kept saying to me that I should go in half with him and I did think about it for a while. I made a proposition that we begin a business and go into it the right way.

That was more than a thought for Mook. He kept insisting that I trust him and give him $10,000.00 and he put up $10,000.00 and since he did construction for work he could easily flip the house. He said that it would make us profitable. Now, this plan sounds good all except the last house he purchased while we were together was a complete whore house and I can't see any different after he barely came in the house now at a reasonable time. I also considered the fact that we were in counseling and we don't have anything together. Would it be foolish to start a business with my husband was the question of a lifetime?

Jealousy

Mook and I relationship was mostly competitive. At this point, since I owned two properties and I also had good credit, I knew that I would be okay once we separate. One of the issues I believe that hurt our relationship was jealousy. Before all the madness and the idea of separation came about, I decided to reward myself for completing a doctoral degree. I knew that I would finish even though it took me way longer than I insisted. So for my reward, I purchase my dream car. Now throughout the years my dream car changed, but for at least ten years it remained the same. I always wanted a Porsche and so one day, I decided I would buy one. I was currently leasing a car with GM and decided near the end of my lease term would be a perfect moment to get my dream car.

Before the purchase I consulted with Mook. I told him how much I wanted the car and that it has always been a dream car for me and that I wanted to get one. I was told by him that I didn't need it. I didn't understand why he couldn't ever be happy for me. He always told me what I didn't need as if he just didn't want me to have anything. Well, unfortunately I went shopping and found a pearl white Porsche Panemera with a peanut butter interior for a bargain steal. I drove home with my Porsche that I named Winter. I had a thing with naming my vehicles and I loved white vehicles. I went through many vehicles with names as well. I had a storm, snowflake, icey, etc. It was something I loved to do because any one that knows me knows I love cars. Cars are like toys for me as an adult so I always buy a new car. It's fun to me and I didn't feel I should stop because how Mook always feel. Every car I purchased he had a problem with. Years back my dream car was a Lexus GS 350 and I bought one cranberry red and he had a problem with that as well. I bought a Dodge Charger and he had an issue with that. So, at this point, it didn't matter if I came home with a Buick LaCrosse which one day I did, and he had a problem with that. So, I decided my Porsche would be the one thing I do for myself regardless of how in the hell Mook feels.

Driving home with this Porsche made me feel

good because that Panemera rides so smooth. I felt like I accomplished something that I wanted almost ten years. Upon driving to the marital home with my new car, I couldn't wait to show him. I even had a spare key for him so he could drive it when he wanted. Now, before I to talk about his response, let me discuss the fact that he just bought a brand new BMW and he was excited to buy. When he wanted his BMW, I joined him on his conquest searching high and low to find him the best deal so that he doesn't over pay. When I found one that was a good deal, I showed him and he went to get that car. I was so happy for him! I put on a dress and some heels and asked him to take me out on a ride in the town. Now fast forward, when I came home that day, I asked him to come outside to see the car. I was like baby I did it! I finally got my dream car! The one I was telling you I wanted! He came out and said it's nice and went back in the house. How did I know he wasn't happy for me was his actions for the next year. Mook refused to step foot in my car and refused to acknowledge the car. Anytime we would go out or have to go to a family function we had to take the BMW.

This was the most foolish shit I ever seen. He specifically told me that he ain't ever getting in the car. He said the reason why is because I didn't need it. I felt as though he didn't need the BMW, but if it was something he wanted to do, then it was fine with me and I support it. Mook made silly ass rules for our relationship that made me despise him all the time. So, for the rest of our relationship he never got into my car. At first it bothered me and we even started taking two cars to family functions because sometimes I refused to get in his car. This was by far the dumbest shit but it is the truth. We drove two cars one year to his mom house for Thanksgiving. But because he smoke cigarettes, I didn't care. I didn't want him smoking in my car anyway. He always smoked in his car and it created a smell that I didn't want in my car. Our relationship at this point was foolish and very immature. I hate to point the finger in this instance, but Mook was the sole reason. You would think our age difference made him more mature. Mook continued to do this throughout our relationship and act as though he was jealous of his own wife. I tried to call my brother in Atlanta for some advice on this matter. My brother was an auto mechanic and he is my baby brother and he knew all about cars. So, when I called my brother Julius he told me the reason why Mook was acting the way he was about the cars was because when I purchased the Porsche after he purchased a BMW, he probably felt small. I told him I wasn't competing I just loved the Porsche Panemera. Julius stated that the Porsche was a way better car than the BMW and I was stuck. I never thought for one minute that it was and that I was just happy to have the car. I didn't want to compete nor did I want to make Mook mad. But, apparently I did. Dating someone from the streets is really hard because their mentality is extremely different.

This wasn't the first thing Mook did like this either. When I purchased the marital home and rented out the first house I ever purchased, it didn't make Mook very happy. Now that I owned two homes and was a landlord he began to feel a certain way that he kept telling me he needed to purchase a second home as well. I was wondering why he was going so hard on obtaining a second home, and it was because I had a second home. I was happy that he wanted to engage in real estate but he began making our relationship a competition. When I got approved for my third property, it was a war in our household. I think the biggest issue is that I might was outgrowing Mook and didn't know. I wasn't conscious of this matter until it was way too late. Mook had an issue with himself that he took out on me. Now he could have joined me but instead he wanted to keep up the BS and have us arguing and fighting over material things. So, when I knew that I was getting done with my Ph.D. soon, anyone could imagine the intensity it created in our home. Mook tried his best to tell me that my degree was a piece of paper. But it was much more than that to me and I couldn't let him downplay my success.

When I got a promotion at my job, Mook didn't want to pay as many bills because he thought I can handle it. What Mook was doing to me was pushing me away from him. He made me look at him differently since he was acting all jealous instead of supportive. I wish he wouldn't act like that but, I learned a valuable lesson about it. Whenever, I had anything extra or I was happy about something, he made sure to put a damper on it. Mook even fixed his mouth to tell me I should just be happy with what I got. That I always wanted way too much and I couldn't just sit down somewhere and just be happy. The answer to that is nope. I have always been a go getter and I am and will always want more. I will never just sit down and be happy when I am blessed with the gift of life. So, what Mook needed was a woman with no goals and that could just down and watch him be successful. I am not that type of woman. I make moves, and most of them are money moves. I am always thinking of my next thing. I was actually thinking of our next thing but he just couldn't jump on the band wagon. He thought that buying cash properties in a poverty neighborhood was the best thing to do. I am not knocking what he wanted to do but while his mind was on that, I was thinking of how I could use my great credit to purchase an airplane, have properties in every state, create royalties, and have different streams of revenue. My mind is much bigger than renting out a few homes in the hood. But, I learned that you cannot carry someone somewhere that they don't want to go. There is an old saying out that reminds me of this. "You can take a horse to a well, but you can't make him drink it"! Enough said!

I have tried to figure out how Mook got this way. He didn't start off this way when we first got together. He was helpful and sweet. He didn't mind or even care about all the things that was destroying us now. It is a mystery of what happened and why the sudden change. I do know I have heard that some women devalue their men so I made sure I was supportive of anything he wanted to do and I treated him well. But, nothing worked. I still catered to Mook even on bad terms. But, no matter what

I did, I began to realize that not only was Mook jealous hearted, Mook just didn't like me. If he liked me or even loved me, he wouldn't be putting me through so much grief. He would be happy for me but, then again, just maybe he isn't happy with himself. Maybe he didn't like his life and how things were going for him. Unless a man is happy with himself, he cannot simply be happy for you. Nor can he be the best man for you. After all, we were definitely on terrible terms anyway and all of this just adds to the already existing issues.

Mook and I had a mountain piled up high of issues. There was nothing left to do anyhow but separate after countless encounters and several heartbreaking incidents. Neither of us had respect for one another anymore and it showed. Our families and friends could see it. Hell, a blind man could see that there was no more love between the two of us anymore. For some reason we didn't separate from this pile of mess we were creating and this fight lasted way too long. I don't even see how we got this far or how I dealt with these relationship restrictions for so long, but I did and I am very regretful.

I began to feel like I wasted my youth in this relationship that was filled with jealousy, lies, insecurities, and on top of all that, it was loveless.

Anytime you're in a relationship with someone and you cannot be happy for your mate, it's a worthless relationship. Mook was envious of my accomplishments and my advantages. What he wanted to do is control everything and since I wouldn't let that happen we were not doing well. I wasn't surprised by him always asking me for money or to use my credit for things he wanted. He once told me if I bought a building for him that if indeed I did it, he would be a more loving husband to me. He told me that he would come in the marital home at a decent time and that he would also spend more time with me and the children.

So, I guess to get a good man out of Mook, you had to pay for it. Well, I don't believe in buying love and I don't believe he fixed his mouth to say some dumb shit like that to me. But, he did! It is crazy to me that I would have to go into debt to get a good husband and that loving me wasn't good enough for him. But, year after year, Mook asked me to buy things for him. Sometimes I would and sometimes I wouldn't. The one thing I did know was I wasn't going to put anything on my credit for him especially since he wasn't showing me through his actions that he wanted to be with me nor did he want to be in our marriage.

So most of my time, I spent thinking and praying. Most of the time, Mook spent time asking me for shit he wouldn't dare do for me. So, I wasn't surprised by his next actions of asking me to go half with him on a property in the hood. But, he never stopped asking me! For some reason he felt like him convincing me to go half on a cheap house or buy him a building was my commitment to him to get him to act right in our marriage. I didn't even want to mess up my credit. I felt since he barely wanted to pay bills in the house, there could be no reason for him to pay a mortgage on a building. Just like any creditor in America, they want to know your ability to pay. His ability to pay was uncertain in his previous actions over the years, so I couldn't even fathom putting that large type of debt on my credit. He wanted a $200k building since he couldn't get it on his own. Crazily, if he was a better husband to me, I probably would have did it. So, now since he was very adamant about me doing something with him, it was hard to answer his next question of going half on a house with him knowing he wouldn't do it for me. The question now was who is more foolish him or me?

Make or Break

Mook asked me over and over again about buying a cash house with him until he decided to take matters in his own hands. I knew this decision I was forced to make would make or break our relationship. After much prayer and following my gut on the entire relationship, I decided not to go ahead with the purchase of a cash house together. I should have told him that I wanted to buy a 2 flat or 3 flat and never do like he always lied to me about. But I just flat out told him no. I did this for several reasons, but the main reason was love. I didn't feel like Mook loved me. Not enough to be committed to the relationship that we were in altogether. I also thought about the fact that I purchased 2 houses without him even wanting or trying to help or put his name on it. I bought the first two houses we lived in together. I was burnt out and tired and I couldn't trust him or follow his lead. At this point he hasn't shown or proven to me that he was capable of carrying all of us on his own. He was not a family man, he didn't want to take trips with the children, just without them, nor did he want to spend game nights with us. So, for the first time, I took a stand and said no. I had no clue that saying no would make or break our relationship, our marriage, but it definitely did.

Mook decided to buy a house on the same exact block as the other house with a friend of his named Eric. Eric was a good friend of his, but it made me sad that he would buy a house with a friend but not with his own wife. Since the house was purchased, there was nothing I could do. I offered Mook a bottle of Remy Martin for yet another accomplishment. I was never a hater, but I started to question this purchase. At first I thought he was buying the house for us to live in but then when he went in with his friend on the purchase of the house, I knew different. I asked him what was his plan and he said he would flip and sell the house in three months. He then asked me if I could handle paying the entire mortgage on the marital house by myself for three months to help him out. HELL NO was my immediate response. I began to do what most women do. I created a mental note and a list of things he wasn't doing.

My task was to write down all the positives and

all the negatives and see if one outweighs the other. Of course the negatives won with flying colors! My main issue with Mook at this point was that he finally purchased a house with someone and it wasn't me. I know he asked me to buy that cash house with him, but that wasn't for us that was for him. The new house I purchased was a family home for us. What I was feeling inside was disgust, betrayal, and pain. What's worst is that house he purchased was making me relive the old whore house. Both houses were on the same street in a very poverty stricken area. You know the area where there are flowers are decorated on trees from someone being killed and there is even a huge funeral home right on the next block. I just couldn't do it and I wanted more for my children. I wanted more for me! What's worst is I wanted more for him! No matter how much I tried to get better for us as a family unit, this man loved the hood and I lost this battle. I felt that house was the death of our marriage. I told him too! I told him you just killed us.

Now that this house was purchased, I had to make a decision. Would I deal with a supplemental whore house? Should I just cut my losses? I was so lost and confused I couldn't see straight. Right when I couldn't think, things could get any worse, it did. The taxes on our marital home went up again! This time the taxes were over $13k and I knew I had to decide to sell or refinance the home. Mook would be gone most of the days now working on the house. He had a point to prove now since this was his first house he purchased for the purpose of a sale. I couldn't worry myself with what he was doing because I was facing an issue at the marital home that was financially straining me, and me alone. Mook started giving me less than half on the mortgage and now the mortgage was $2000 a month.

The month that he decided to give me only $500, I was ready for him to move. I end up cutting the cable off, stop cooking so much, and started leaving the house as soon as he came in drunk. I didn't want to be bothered and now I checked out of the relationship. Most of his time was spent either getting drunk or working on the other house so we didn't have much of a friendship, let alone a marriage. We spent days without talking on the phone or texting. I was starting to realize that we were slowly separating. As time went on Mook was still not paying bills nor communicating with me much. He continued to sleep in the basement and my once then marriage, turned into a roommate situation.

One day Mook was outside smoking his cigarettes like normal, and was on the cell phone with his friend. Since we had an alarm on the house, the ring doorbell was installed, and I knew that I could listen in on his very private conversation. This conversation was yet a make or break moment for me as well. He was on the phone with a friend of his named Richard and was asking him to meet him at a car wash so they can wash their cars together. Mook stayed trying to get away and find a way out the house. It was Saturday morning and he was trying to find something to do. Richard didn't want to wash his car with him because he was busy. But he asked what he was doing later that night. Mook response was he wasn't sure but he would definitely hang out with him and the guys especially if I get on his mutha fucking nerves. He continued on by telling Richard that he was sick of me and was tired of me and my shit. I couldn't believe what I heard. I knew then that my marriage that I once knew, was over.

I decided to buy a journal and began to write. I wrote down how in the hell could I get myself out this marriage, while still trying get my oldest child through her senior year without disruption. While Mook was busy and every time he left the house, I would take care of business. I would make business calls, write in my journal, and consult with my attorney. I also had a friend who I call my sister who lived in Atlanta who was recently divorced. So, I called her so she coach me through my divorce. Her name was Jaz. Jaz knew every single thing about divorce like she was an expert. Her advice was invaluable and I couldn't have made it look so easy if she didn't help me along the way. I wanted to be extremely strategic if this was what I was going to really do. I prayed every night and made sure I hugged and kissed my children because I knew that this separation would be extremely difficult for all of us. The only way out was through God so I depended on him heavily. I planned how the separation would look for me and the girls from the beginning stages to the completion stages so I can be well prepared.

As time went on Mook began to get verbally abusive towards me. I was every bitch in the book. The disrespect didn't hurt my feelings as much until one day when we began to argue he kept threatening me saying I ain't going do shit and if I don't like what he what he was doing, go file a divorce. When he did this to me, I felt like a child and began to want my father. I knew if my father knew he was talking to me like this, he would fly in town all the way from Maryland to beat his ass. My father was a military man and was a former US Marshall. My father was also the type of man that treated his daughters like princesses. So, I knew better and I wanted better, but unfortunately, I did not get better. I was 1 of 7 children my father has. There are 3 girls and four boys and all of us are grown but my little sister Mandy who is 16.

Getting back on track, anytime I try to talk to Mook about either what time he comes in if at all, or even smoking in the house, he would respond with, I am going to do what in the hell I want to do. He would ask me time and time again what I want to do about all these complaints. It was like he kept pushing my buttons and forcing my hand to file a divorce. One argument got so bad that he had the audacity to tell me I am going to get bitch slapped. That was the very last time I argued to that nature. I went into our walk in closet and broke down and cried. I cried, cried, and then I prayed. I asked God to help me. As I pleaded with God I told him, I simply cannot do this anymore and I want out.

The very next day, Mook left for church to get

his son baptized without my acknowledgement and to my surprise his entire family attended my church for the ceremony. Now I was extremely close to his family. I was disturbed that neither my children nor I was invited but I didn't take it out on the family. I took it out on Mook. I was livid to find out that Mook baby mama and her family was also in attendance and no one mentioned it to me. That day changed me. I decided I wouldn't attend another family event and guess what I didn't. I didn't celebrate no more holidays with them nor did I call them anymore. I felt betrayed but I'm not confrontational so I never really mentioned it. I felt like if I am only invited to selected events, then I wouldn't want to be invited to any. Period! I loved Mook son like he was my own and being that I had 3 girls, he was the only son I had. I wasn't petty though, and I called his son to tell him how proud I was of him for his Christianity and his new transitions in life.

Right when I thought everything couldn't get any worst, it did. Mook went out the next week and didn't come home until extremely late. This time I woke up out my sleep at about 6:00 am and he wasn't home. I checked the alarm cameras to see if he came in and left early to go work on the house that he and his friend just purchased but this was not the case. I had been so busy studying to get my Ph.D. that I never thought of going to look for him. I did go out sometimes but mainly I stayed home with the children and studied. Because my oldest was almost 18, I went into her room and told her I'll be right back.

I hopped in my car and traveled to all his friends' homes. I started at Richard's home, Eric's home, and even his best friend Romeo home. I went to his sister home, his mother home, and even his brother Gill's new apartment. Gill recently just moved into an apartment and I remember him asking me to fix his resume and it had his address on it. Since I had never been, I went into my email to retrieve it. Mook was nowhere to be found. Anyone from Chicago knows what to do next and yes I did it too. I called 311 to have Central Bookings check to see if he was arrested. The police departments and everyone looked for him and no one could find where Mook was located. The operator kept telling me calm down and I kept saying he got to be cheating or dead because there is no way he isn't nowhere to be found. I also drove around all the spots he typically hang at as well before I realized that I should just go home.

I got back home around 8:45 am and he still

wasn't home. Mook came home at 9:16 am and there was no more talking. I asked Mook to grab his shit and go! He tried to tell me he was at Eric's house. I told him I went over there and Eric's son, Eric, Jr. answered the door and said Mook was not there. Mook told the biggest lie of all, and that was he fell asleep in Eric's garage in the dead smack of winter! I couldn't take anymore lies, and I was officially done with that man and all his shenanigans. I asked Mook to move out of the house. Mook didn't want to leave and it definitely wasn't easy to get him out the house he hated being in surprisingly.

Take Out the Trash

All that planning I was doing when he wasn't home was now in full effect. Fortunately, I was about to finally graduate with my Ph.D. and I couldn't even be happy and celebrate because my personal life was so shitty. I was 34 years old now, and 15 years invested into a failing relationship. Mook was now 41 and what we once had was now over. I had 23 people coming to my graduation and so I had to put on a smiling face. I uninvited Mook to my graduation due to us now being separated. I was close to his children and still wanted them to come, but he told me that they couldn't go if he wasn't. Although his children were both 19 years old at this time, I respected his wishes. His children were not twins by the way, he had two children when he was 20 years old, two months apart with two different women. But, that was before me so I wasn't concerned, but maybe I should have been.

It was a few months before my graduation when

I gave Mook eight weeks to move. I felt that it was fair to give him time since he claimed he didn't have anywhere to go and he didn't want to move back into his mother home. At that time, I decided that we should sleep separate and he agreed so he continued to sleep in the basement. I started helping him pack his clothes out of the walk in closet by putting his things nicely in a box and labeling them. Sometimes he would ask me to talk, but I was all talked out actually, I was mad as hell. I think I was actually madder at myself than him. I was trying to figure out how in the hell did he get my entire youth from me and I allowed all the bs to happen.

I printed the divorce papers to review and it kind of broke me down. The craziest part was I was looking forward to weekends so that he can go out and I can plan and execute my next move. But when Fridays came, he didn't go out anymore. I actually would walk down in the basement and ask him like what time you going out? I think for the first time he began to worry what I was doing while he was away. I never cheated on him, so I don't know why he would feel this way. I actually never cheated on anyone I been in a relationship with. I just feel like If I want someone else, I will leave you alone and then pursue the next person I am interested in because I was too busy to try and keep up with multiple men. It was also not a good look for my three girls to have mommy with all these men.

I decided I would just wait until he goes to work to plan and execute my next moves. Crazily he stopped going to work as well. I was furious that I couldn't get a break or get rid of him. He also stopped working on the house that he and his friend Eric just purchased. I was thinking to myself like now that I have completely checked out of this relationship, this dude want to stay in the house. Fifteen years I been begging him to slow down and spend quality time with me and the children and he would never do it. If he did it even once, it would be a full surprise to all of us. So, I had to plan on my own on what I needed to do and how I wanted to do things.

As I started planning how I am going to get this next year over with by myself, I realized that it could put me in a financial bind. I knew that he wasn't paying much but the little he was paying was helping especially with my oldest graduating out of a private high school. So I increased my two main credit cards to $10,000 limits so that I can have access to an emergency fund just in case. As a mother I didn't want to interrupt my oldest last year in high school, although I was already going through the beginning stages of a divorce.

In the meantime, Mook started buying flowers for me every single day saying he wanted to work things out. This is by far the craziest thing to me at this point. I did consider at first, I am not going to lie. But I wanted Mook out the house because now I was paying the full mortgage all alone and all the bills too. I changed the gas bill out of his name and put it in my name. Sadly that was all the separating we had to do in 15 years! As time went on I began to be angry as hell and started taking all the pictures down off the wall if he was in it. It was like something in me snapped and I had no control how furious I was with him especially with all the time I wasted. I kept asking him when he is leaving. He kept saying soon and that he had to find somewhere to go because he refused to go live with his mom. I kept insisting he rent an apartment or something. I was no longer cooking dinner period and we were not being intimate either. We didn't talk on the phone or text each other and weeks had went by. After 4/8 weeks went by, I could no longer live with Mook. I wanted him out immediately. I couldn't stand to even look at him. The pain I was feeling was so surreal and it hurt me that he was still in the house. Now at this point he was living off me because he no longer was paying. So, when it was time to pay again I told him to leave because it is not fair that he isn't paying anything.

Mook finally gathered his belongings and left. The moment he left I was relieved, but I was still very angry. I woke up the next day to a very long message from him saying he wanted to start over. It made me emotional and I began to cry. I told him maybe we can go to counseling. I never hurt anyone in my life but his message, showed me he was truly hurt. So, guess what I signed us up for counseling now for the third time and we went consistently session after session for about 4 weeks. At the end of I think it was our 5th or 6th session, Mook told the counselor that he would never return to the marital home ever again. That if I wanted to be with him I would have to buy us a 3rd house. Yes, that negro said I would have to buy it! I asked him at counseling where he live and to my surprise he moved into the house he and Eric purchased. Listening to him tell me that did a few things to me internally.

It was a pause moment for me to reflect again. I had to think to myself and say did he buy this house to move away from me from the get go, or did he truly have nowhere to go and he saw this as an opportunity to live rent free in an abandoned house. I tried to think of the best case scenario and not have such negative thoughts. I was wondering when he asked me to pay the mortgage for three months while he get the house together, was it for him to leave me? I mean he wasn't happy either with the relationship which shows by his absence. The real issue here was trust and it was clear I didn't trust him at all.

When we departed our last counseling session, I acted like I wanted to go to the bathroom when he walked out to talk to the counselors alone. This was the best decision I ever made because the male and female counselors sat me down to talk to me about Mook. What the counselors shared with me confirmed somewhat I already knew. But I listened anyway. The counselors shared with me that Mook has something deeply rooted inside of him that he need to deal with that has nothing to do with me. They said they have been counselors for several years, and they can see from our relationship issues, that there is no love left and they are not sure if there was any at all in the first place. They also told me that they thought Mook was extremely immature for his age and that he doesn't know how to love me correctly because he wasn't shown. They asked me was his father not in his life and I told them that he wasn't. They told me that there is no way a few counseling sessions could help us. That is was advisable for us to figure out what we were, before we returned. We never returned because we weren't nothing and we had nothing left.

I left that counseling session feeling like there was no hope. I went to God and asked for his help. I asked him to give me some obvious signs that I should walk away from my marriage, and I got the biggest signs of all. No communication at all from anyone. Not him, his mother, his brother, his sister, or his children reached out to me. After all I have done for everyone, helping, and being there, I officially had silence. Now I don't know why I expected any different, but I did expect to hear from the children. I have bent over backwards for the children providing them everything I gave my own. But in life you take losses and I was ready to start taking my losses. In the end I told him that him buying that house will either make or break us. It definitely did break us and now it was time for me to get myself together and move forward.

The Aftermath

Graduation morning hit, and I was ready to finally walk across the stage and earn my stripes. I have been waiting on this day for eight years and after receiving eleven denials, I was glad that the twelfth was a success. As my family and I gathered for this enormous accomplishment, I began to feel a void. I felt like I might have missed Mook a little, but every time I thought about the fact that I was about to walk across a stage and graduate with his last name and put a Dr. on it, it pissed me off. Not only did he not help me with my degree, he had so much negativity about me earning it, so I just didn't want him there anyway. He kept telling that earning your doctorate degree ain't nothing but a piece of paper. He wanted to discourage me from getting my degree by telling me that I wasn't earning enough money for the Master's degree I earned previously. Mook could really be so demeaning at times. But, I didn't want him to ruin this moment from me so I didn't. There is no way his uneducated ass knew anything about a degree. He has no degree. So, he couldn't understand.

Funny thing is a few weeks back I decided to take some road trips and flights and ran into one of my male friends I known from back in the day and we began chatting on the phone. So, when graduation day approached he sent me a very nice encouraging message that helped uplift my spirits. He always liked me I knew but because I was in a relationship I would never give him the time of day. Although I wasn't going to be with him and we lived in separate states, it was nice to have someone to talk to, receive compliments from, and even hang out with a couple times.

When I walked across the stage, I had a ceremony dance as I was proud of myself. I was also blessed to have both my parents and both my step parents present along with 3 of my brothers and my 2 sisters. It has been a long time before my siblings and I have come together and to have 6/7 present, was a true blessing. My graduation was in Tampa, Florida and boy did we have a ball. We went out to eat and the siblings all went to a strip club to celebrate together. It was a blessing to be able to hang like that. I will never forget the support. My best friend attended my graduation as well. Her name is Nya. I have two best friends and my other best friend Cara was just relocating to Washington, DC so she couldn't attend. But she attend everything all the time and I was so happy on her relocation and proud of her new accomplishments.

We all stayed in Tampa for 4 days hanging out and having fun. Having a full family present with nieces and nephews made my time go by fast. I appreciated everyone for coming and no one asked me not one time where was Mook. Thank God! I think my family was sensing it was an issue so before we left, I sent out a message to them and let them know he wasn't attending and that we are no longer together. I pretty much wanted to just let my parents know and that is it. When I came home from the graduation Mook purchased some balloons that said DR and some flowers and left it in the house for me. I told him thank you and it reminded me that I needed to change the locks and the alarm code. It also reminded me that I needed to deactivate his alarm access as well.

I decided to fill my life up with vacations to pass time. I would work during the week and travel every weekend for 4 weeks to allow a month time to pass to prevent me from going back to him. I travel to

Atlanta the next weekend, then to Arizona the next weekend, then to Tennessee. I wanted to stay away from Illinois where we lived so it can prevent me from going back and forth to that situation that I knew for sure wouldn't work out. So now the time I needed was space to heal. Time to get my thoughts together. I didn't realize I been under him so long that I didn't know what to do with myself.

I began to clean and pack up the house. I owned 2 homes in my name and so my plan was to sell both and move out of state myself. So I put both houses on the market. The marital home went fast! Only after being listed for 3 hours I was flooded with contracts and the contract I selected actually closed in less than 60 days. I end up finding a short term lease apartment in Indiana to move right into so that I don't have to move into the other house that was on the market just to move right back out. I also charged up my credit cards to keep everything normal in the house for my oldest last year. I didn't want her to be affected by this new change. My plan was to file my taxes and repay all debt and save money to buy a new house. Everything that I planned while Mook was outside with his friends getting drunk worked out great! I sold all the furniture in the house that I didn't want to take to Texas. Texas was the state

I decided I would start my life over. I thought more sunny days would help me be in a better mood. I also moved into the apartment and transferred the children out of their old school. I sent my oldest to college and now it was time to file for my divorce from Mook. Since I hadn't heard from him this made it even easier.

Making Things Final

In order to not worry the children for such a transition, I got them a puppy. The puppy is a Chihuahua mixed with Shiatzu and I named her Houston after the town we wanted to move. I figured the puppy would cause a distraction since the girls all were used to him being around. The puppy kept them really busy and with all the new responsibilities, I could finally bring up the courage to walk into the courthouse and finally file for divorce. I will never forget how I felt when I got to the courthouse. I felt relieved and I felt that I was finally going to correct some of the things I should have been corrected. I picked up Nya and she rolled with me for the first court hearing. Nya kept reminding me that this is for the betterment of my life. That for the last few years she never seen me so unhappy. Nya listened to me a million times tell her how Mook was acting and not coming home or spending quality time with me. Nya reminded me over and over again that this isn't love. She wanted to see me happy and that was all she cared about. I wish I did too back then and not waste so much of my time.

I can say that getting to the first court hearing, I was nervous. Nya kept telling me that Mook ain't showing up for court. I had hope that he would and we can begin getting this over with. Well that was wishful thinking. Mook missed this court date and also the next three dates thereafter. He refused to show up and grant me my divorce. I tried to send him text messages and place phone calls but by now I hadn't heard from him in months. The judge began to become irritated and called him herself. He didn't answer her calls either. The judge gave me a contact of hers to hire a private investigator to get him served since he refused to answer for the sheriff.

The private investigator actually served Mook at the whore house #2 the same day I hired them. I was extremely excited that he got served. If anyone filed for divorce, you would know that you cannot get a divorce until the respondent is served. So, I at least accomplished one goal. But I had no clue it was going to be like pulling teeth to get Mook to the court house. In the meantime, I was finally getting settled in my apartment in Indiana when I received a message from my very first boyfriend Jay. I didn't expect a message from Jay and I haven't heard from him for at least 11 years when he messaged me to see how things were going. I knew back then that he wanted more than I could offer him so when he reached out to me I told him that I was in a relationship and that I couldn't talk with him nor meet with him. He was very respectful of my relationship back then. But to hear from him again hit me differently this time.

To My Surprise

et me take a minute to explain who Jay was to me. Jay was my very first friend and my very first boyfriend when my mom moved us to a new neighborhood when I was in eighth grade. As I had been in the same school with all my friends and wanted to graduate with my best friend Nya, but my mom got married and we moved. I didn't want to move, but it was nothing I could do as I was a teen. When I moved to the new neighborhood it was cool because my cousin Sweetie lived out there and we would attend the same school. So, I did know someone. Jay was one of the first people who liked me and it was probably because I was the new girl. Either way, he was so sweet to me. He would write me love letters, buy me candy, and bring me flowers.

He was one of the leading players on the basketball team and I was a cheerleader so we were one of the cutest couples. One day we were hanging out and we had a half of day at school and he invited me to come chill with him at his parent's house. I went to chill with him because my mother didn't know we had a half of day and on that day, Jay took my virginity. I couldn't believe I actually had sex at the young age of 14 but I did. Jay never told a sole about what happened to us and it was our secret to keep. I don't know a single young boy who wouldn't want bragging rights, but Jay didn't. Closer to graduation, we went on a trip to Atlanta with the school and it was like we were on a vacation together. I hung out in his hotel room and we walked around all hugged up on each other the entire trip. If my mother knew this, she definitely wouldn't have even let me go I'm sure. We did not engage in any sexual activity while we were on the trip, just kissing, hugging, and a little rubbing on each other. Unfortunately, his family was moving and I knew our time was short.

Depending on where you live in our neighborhood, you would go to high school with only two options. Unfortunately, we lived on two different sides of the neighborhood and we knew that we would separate. It was very sad to me that we would separate. We spent our last night out in a Rolls Royce limo with friends going downtown after our dinner dance. We had a ball that night and that was the last night we would hangout. After graduation, we went our separate ways and his family moved him out of state. Jay was all but a memory until now.

So, when he reached out to me in my dm on Facebook, I was pleasantly surprised. His message stated that he was so proud of me and all my accomplishments. He also asked me how was married life and didn't want to be intrusive but he wanted to know why Mook wasn't in any of my graduation pictures for my Ph.D. These were great questions, but I couldn't lie to him and I told him that we were separated. I also told him that I filed for divorce. I asked him what happened to his children mother as well. He completely avoided the questions I had at first.

Days went by without speaking to Jay because he didn't answer my questions and now I didn't have time to play with no one after wasting an entire 15 damn years. I didn't have 15 damn seconds to offer anyone not serious or who wanted to play. I thought about him a lot and started going through his Facebook pictures to see what he was up to and what he has been doing with his life. Jay was very consistent though. He definitely hit me back for more time. This time he asked could he facetime me so we could talk and that he just wanted to see me. I agreed to the communication because I had nothing else to do anyway.

To my surprise, Jay looked the exact same as he did when we were 14 years old except he was fully grown, his body looked like one of the Gods, and he was extremely handsome. All my old feelings came back immediately as he greeted me with his pearly white teeth saying hello to me. All I could say to myself is this man is all types of fine and our chemistry was something crazy ridiculous. We talked on that Facetime call for about 2 hours catching up and sharing our life time stories for the last 20 years we missed with each other.

Talking to Jay became my new addiction as he was very smart, very intellectual, and successful. Jay had accomplished so much in his life already. He owned three properties paid off cash, he had a work van paid off, a BMW 750Li paid off cash, a Chrysler 300 paid off cash, his own Semi Truck paid off cash, and his own business. I was beyond impressed with what he had done in the 20 years we weren't speaking. I couldn't help but be proud. I asked him where he lived and he told me he lived in New Jersey. I was like wow! You have done very well for yourself to only be 34 years old. So in the back of my mind, this man was not only handsome, but was very successful.

Jay was very persistent and he was very honest and clear cut about what is going on with him. He told me that he wanted me back in his life and that for the last 20 years, I been on his mind and he never felt like he did again since we separated. This was far-fetched to me at first, but as time progressed it was true. Jay is a Libra and apparently since I am an Aquarius, we were a perfect match according to astrology. I never knew someone so caring and so sweet that his conversation and his honesty drew me closer to him. His tone and character was nothing I ever seen. He was so sweet and told me he wanted me to come see him. I didn't want to see him this soon as I was still married. I told him he can send for me. It was almost his 35th birthday so I knew I could at least have a sit down with him. Guess what? That is exactly what I did. When I walked into the same room with this man I haven't seen in 20 years, I thought it would be weird but it wasn't.

Jay was nervous and had a bit of anxiety but upon seeing me, I walked right up to him and hugged him real tight. I missed him very much and our daily conversations had built up many more emotions as well. As soon as the hug was over, we kissed.

It was a peck nothing more but it was on the lips. We sat in each other presence for 8 hours straight before we realized we didn't eat a thing just talked and laughed and held hands. It was an amazing conversation. When it was time for me to depart Jay and go back to the hotel room to get some rest before we hung out the next day, we decided to kiss again but this time it was a French kiss and it felt like we been together forever.

We met up the next day and talked for about 6 hours holding hands and kissing. I talked to him about being about being abstinent and that I wasn't having sex with anyone because not only was I still married, I wanted a mental connection with someone over a sexual one. I learned my lesson the last time in previous relationships. I wanted him to know that I wouldn't have sex with anyone until I was married. This might seem farfetched but I was so serious. Jay told me that he thought this was a great idea especially since he wants to get married to me. Yes, he said he wanted to marry me only after being back reunited for a few months.

Let me break this down. Jay stated to me that he don't need 10 years to figure out what he wants, and any man that needed 10 years, wasn't sure anyway and wasting time. He told me that he prayed every night for God to bring him someone and didn't know it would be me but it was. Jay grew up in the church. His mother and father actually own their own church. I've attended this church a couple of times and I love it there. His uncle own a church as well in Flint, Michigan. Jay was really religious and we prayed together every night. For the first time in my life I truly believe that I found my soul mate. I wanted to find a man that was God fearing and wanted more out of life than just staying in one place. I told Jay of my plans to relocate and to my surprise he told me he will move to Texas too if it meant he could spend the rest of his life with me.

Jay started to turn into a dream. Months went by and I visited with him once a month to eat and chill and have non-sexual communication. We began to get closer talking every day, all day, and all night. Jay gave me everything I could ever wanted by being attentive, loving, and caring. I started to think to myself was I blocking my own blessings with Mook and staying with him all that time for no reason apparently? Jay was open to giving me access to everything and gave me keys to everything including his heart. He gave me keys to the houses, cars, vans, semi-trucks, and even added me to his bank account. He wanted me to know how serious he was with me. He loves surprising me. He got me my first ever chinchilla and got me these Steve Madden combat boots I acted like a baby about.

Anything and everything I want, I can have and he will make a way. He always remind me that I can have whatever I want from him and that whatever he has is mine. He wasn't lying. My family wasn't so sure about everything about us moving so quickly at first, but they started to see his genuine heart. Jay surprised me with many unexpected things like sending me money through cash app, sending edible arrangements to my job and balloons, and writing me love letters weekly. I never seen love like this before and I have never been happier. Jay has genuine love for me. One day he decided to make a promise to me that he would be true to me and wait for me until marriage by getting my name tattooed on his ring finger. I couldn't believe he did that! This man was head over heels for me and for once it felt good. He was here for me throughout some very hard times I was facing and I couldn't believe how attentive he was. He text and call me all day long. He wanted to be sure I was ok all the time and he even asked about my children. He began sending them gifts too. I knew things became real when he set up a meeting at his parents church for me to meet his children, his grand-parents, and even his baby mama. He explained to me that everyone need to know who I am to him because I will be his wife. He let go of all his little female friends and made it known to everyone that I am the Queen B in his life. What a breath of fresh air!

His family was very accepting of me as well. He has two living brothers, one deceased brother, and a sister that I love so much! He also has a sister in law named Ms. Kitty that is the bomb and she has the same since of humor as I do. Everyone children accepted my children in as their own and we immediately became family. All of our children play together and now are cousins. I hate to say it, but won't God do it!!! I am forever grateful and it only been almost nine months since we started back talking. Jay was patient while I went through a bickering and ugly divorce with Mook.

I did finally get to court with Mook to finalize the divorce and this cat came to court with his wedding ring on and a whole bunch of clothes. It was like he was attending a funeral with the black blazer, black glasses, and black hat, but also attending a St. Patrick's Day celebration with a green sweater and green shoes. I was actually embarrassed walking in the court room because he was over and under dressed. But it was finally no longer my concern. I prayed for him that day that he finds whatever it is he needed in the city and that we can end things amicably. I never wanted him to be alone, I just didn't want him anymore and I had no reason to want him. I am sure that he can now be in his element in the hood and enjoy whatever that looks like. It took five hours for him to sign the papers and to have our court hearing, but I was glad that this was the last day I ever see him, and trust me Jay was happier than me.

Independent Lessons

There was so many lessons that happened through my relationship experiences. I wasted 15 years with someone who wasn't even ready for marriage. I was very embarrassed to even discuss what I went through due to exposure of my friends and family. I didn't want anyone to judge me knowing that I dealt with so much from an underserving man. What was worst is that my father paid for my entire wedding. I often times tried really hard to make things work and there were so many red flags. I worked really hard to not be embarrassed because I cared so much of what others think.

I am hoping by reading what I went through it could help another woman out who is stuck in a situation like I was and save them some heart ache and pain. Even with 3 degrees earning my Bachelors of Arts, my Masters in Public Administration, and my Ph.D. in Public Policy & Administration, owning multiple properties, multiple cars, being a dynamic mom, and having a successful career, I still failed in choosing the right man. How could I be successful in every way but when it comes to relationships, I was foolish? This is not my first failed relationship. The relationship with my oldest father failed as well. I had some small little non-committal relationships in between but truthfully I spent so much time in a failed marriage that it wasn't worth speaking on the other relationships as much. I gave up on myself while I was being married to Mook.

What I wanted to understand is how in the hell did I expect a man from the streets to be a man of the house? It is kind of like turning a hoe into a housewife. It doesn't work! I expected Mook to grow up because I did. Most women mature way faster than men anyways. This man had a seven year age advantage on me and still it didn't help. I had an idea in my head that I shouldn't date men my age because they are immature but looks like age doesn't have anything to do with it.

No matter how hard I tried to provide a since of normal life with a nice house, nice neighborhood, and a family life, not all people want that. You can't take someone out of their element and expect a full change. It took me a long time to realize this.

I also learned that it is nothing wrong with Mook either. Everyone has a limit and apparently I was too young to know mine. Mook was a young man who grew up without a father and although his mom did the best she could, the streets raised him. The way I which he thought was street based. The way he wanted to do things wasn't bad, it just wasn't the way I wanted to do things or how I was raised. We wasn't a match from the beginning and whoever came up with the saying that opposites attract, they are a liar. Opposites have divided relationships and that is about it!

If I had to offer some advice to the women of today, I would say, find you someone who has a lot in common with you. Do not marry someone who doesn't value marriage, family life, ready to put God first in your relationship, or you have a bad history to build. Be sure to discuss everything you want in life even in the future. Share your 5 year plan, 10 year plan, and even 20 year plan. If the man you are with doesn't have one, RUN! Nothing will ever get better and you will never get over the things that has happened wrongly between you two. You will build a full wall of resentment and be mad at yourself like I was. Pay attention to red flags, they are red for a reason. If you do not respect yourself, neither will your mate. If he doesn't respect you, neither will his friends. Don't give a man an ultimatum just leave, it will save you pain, heartache, and money.

The real lesson behind this entire book is if you are in a relationship with someone and you are operating independently and not as a team, you are independently foolish. Which means you can be very successful at many things but you still are being foolish when it comes to men. If a man has cheated on you and you have accepted, you have also let him know that his behavior is okay. We women are so scared of being alone that we forget that it might be something greater on the other side but you can't get to it because of your fear of losing, a loser. In fact, you already lost! There is nothing wrong with space either. Taking time alone to yourself to find yourself. I know this sounds easier said than done, but it is a good way to learn yourself and clear your mind. I am living witness that you can do it.

It got to the point where I didn't even know what type of food I liked because I was so busy pleasing a man. I didn't know what type of television shows I liked or what my favorite color is because I operated in a manner that my man was everything. That was by far the biggest mistake. There is nothing wrong with giving your all in a relationship to the right man. But why give it to someone who is not committed solely to you and the cause of the relationship? I know that it sounds sad, but if your man has done a lot of things wrong to you and you know you are still hurting from it, please think. Take time to yourself and think. I was told by my friend Tangie, that if you take away all of the fairy tale and the endless possibilities, ask yourself what do you have today?

Today you will find out that you have a no good, aint shit man, which has done several things wrong to you. This man has done so much that you could build a grocery list of things like I did. Then, when you finally see everything for what it really is, decide what you want to do about it. Do you really see your future in the situation you are currently dealing with? Did you cut off your family and friends for this man and are you in isolation because he is too controlling or antisocial? Has he put his hands on you? Does he call you out your name? Is he disrespectful? Are you first in his life or last? Whatever secret you are holding onto, will forever be in your heart. You don't even have to tell anyone because I didn't until now. It takes time to be brave enough to tell everyone in the world the truth. It take some growth and maturity to sit in front of an audience and allow yourself to be judged or worst, criticized.

Just remember that things in a relationship doesn't get better over time, it gets worst. Getting married doesn't change a thing especially if you are begging for a ring. I was told don't shit change at the altar by Mook several times and trust me, it doesn't. The altar made everything worse, because he didn't care enough about marriage. Looking into someone childhood is essential. Marriage counseling is essential. I have tried everything in my power to look smart and intelligent in front of people but my deepest secret in life was that I was relationship foolish. There are many good women in this world that becomes attracted to what we think is a good looking man with swag. Trust me it doesn't pay off. Looks mean nothing, but their heart and their intentions mean everything. If you are unsure, don't do nothing! Pray, let go, and let GOD!

Think about if you are a mother and what your children will see. Does every man need to meet your children? Does the man you have now engage with your children? Or is he the type of man who really just want to be with you and the children just get a hello, goodbye, and maybe some candy? Does he know your children favorite foods or books?

I promise that women over look everything. I do know by looking at my father and my brothers that there are good men out here. Some men are not ready for what you might be ready for and no matter how hard you try to force it, you will fail!

I know I should have been left my situation the moment I bought my first house, or the hospital even with the chicks, or even the whore house dilemma. But I stayed and dealt with emotional and verbal abuse by a non-deserving man. I should have left before the 10 years passed that we weren't married and I am not sure how I dealt with all that time. The only thing I can think of is time. I have been giving good advice to my best friends Cara, Nya, and even my friend Tangie and many others that has helped them significantly but, I couldn't even help myself. I went through a very dark moment in my life where I felt alone and that I had no one but in reality, I did it all to myself.

I had to learn to treat people how they treat me. I learned that I was treating a man better than I ever been treated. I know that as women we want to be the exception to the rule. We want to feel like we are the reason a man has changed. In reality, a man will change if and only if they want. If they don't want to change, they won't. They might even act like they changed, but trust me it is temporarily. The truth will always reveal itself. There were so many times, I felt like I changed a man. I lied to myself and us as women lie and deceive our own mind more than men. We are so stuck on what could be or how he may come around and never do.

I do know that a man that has been through some failed relationships might begin a new relationship and be a completely changed man, but it is only because they have finally matured. But only when they are ready and not when we are ready for them. My ex-husband will probably learn from the mistakes of all his relationships and be a better man for the next woman and I am actually happy for him. Although it was a 15 year lesson for the both of us, I am sure the lessons learned will improve us in the near future. I learned so much from that relationship that I am now grateful. Sometimes taking out the trash, which means cleaning up the mess you made, is the best thing to do.

I am enjoying my new beginnings and getting to know my new man and talking about life, politics, and love. We have so much in common, it is crazy! I never knew that someone the same age as myself could be so advance. Jay has so much to offer and is teaching me so much. I always thought I had a hard time following someone or investing with someone. I think the biggest issue for me was believing in someone who had no idea what they were doing or even having a solid plan. Upon my first conversation after making things official with Jay, his first sentence was I have a five year plan for us. I want to sit down with you and talk about it. His first question to me was how much student loan debt you have so I can pay it off for you? This man has created a solid plan with paying off my student loans in two years' time. I already feel like I am on a better path.

Financial freedom is what Jay preach to me on every day and before now, I was irritated by this. I was irritated because I didn't see the plan because there wasn't one. Jay has so much under his name attached to no debt it is ridiculous. His mind is of brilliance and I am even honored to be with him. He comes from a full family of entrepreneurs and no one in his immediate family work for anyone. They all have solid businesses. Jay's parents are still together and this speaks volumes in itself. He has a mindset of being married one time and one time only. He speaks of cherishing and loving me forever in front of everyone and any one. I don't have to fight with him because I already won. I can have whatever I want. I didn't think there was any men left like this but there is and I would have never known had I stayed in an unhealthy ass marriage. I have no ill will for my ex but I can honestly thank him for filling a space that allowed me to grow and learn to become an even better woman than I was before. I am truly myself when I am with Jay. We are able to plan everything because we are planners. We have planned our next five years which includes children, building a house from the ground up, and opening multiple businesses.

Naturally I am silly, I love to dance, debate, and research things. Jay is the exact same. I have honestly met my soul mate and I have been healed of the independent foolishness that I suffered from for many years. The good thing about Jay is he has patience and is not pressuring me. We have made a promise to one another and decided to both get name tattoos on our fingers. We do plan to get married in a couple years' time. If it was up to him, we would be married already. But he is allowing me time since I am recently divorced, I also tattooed his name on my ring finger. There is so much more to come from this reunification of us. We have received so much support from our friends and family. I went from being independently foolish to independently loved. Looks like my independence doesn't bother Jay and I can remain myself. He prefers to add to me instead of take away. He gave me a new meaning of independence. Now independence means us as a couple on our own independently. If I can do this anyone can. Moving on was by far the best thing that ever happen to me. I don't have any bad history, and I can now control my narrative. So, now my new journey begin. Stay tuned.

Meet the Author

D r. Erika Jones was born in the south side of Chicago. Throughout her childhood, she moved around a lot living in mostly the suburbs. She became a mom at the early age of 16. Being a teen mom motivated her to push for success. She skipped a grade in high school going from a sophomore to a senior, and went straight to college. She received her Bachelors of Art in 2007, her Master's in Public Administration in 2009, and her Ph.D. in Public Policy & Administration in 2018. She is raising 3 beautiful girls. She spends her spare time advocating for social injustice, writing, and reading books. Her career of choice is Finance/School Administration and has been for the last eleven years. What she aspires in life is to be happy.

Keynote

A young, successful African American woman who accomplished so much in life early on in her career. But, suffered severely in her relationship being foolish until she reached her breaking point.

Made in the USA
Las Vegas, NV
02 February 2022

42935913R00069